PRINCEWILL LAGANG

Healthy Hearts, Happy Homes: A
Christian Marriage Handbook

# Contents

# 1

# The Foundation of Love

Introduction

Welcome to "Healthy Hearts, Happy Homes: A Christian Marriage Handbook." This book is designed to help couples build and maintain strong, Christ-centered marriages that thrive on love, faith, and commitment. In this first chapter, we will explore the essential foundation upon which every lasting Christian marriage is built – love.

The Christian Perspective on Love

In Christian marriages, love is not just a feeling; it's a sacred commitment. It is often described as "agape love," a selfless and sacrificial love that reflects the love of Christ for His church. In Ephesians 5:25, the Apostle Paul writes, "Husbands, love your wives, just as Christ loved the church and gave himself up for her." This sets the tone for the love that should permeate every Christian marriage.

Understanding Love's Components

To build a healthy Christian marriage, it's crucial to understand the different components of love:

1. Agape Love: This is the foundation, selfless love that seeks the best for your spouse, even when it requires sacrifice.

2. Philia Love: This represents the love between friends, the deep companionship that makes a marriage not just about romance but also about building a lasting friendship.

3. Eros Love: This is the romantic and passionate love that initially draws two people together.

4. Storge Love: The affectionate, nurturing love between family members. In a Christian marriage, this love extends beyond the couple to embrace a broader family and community.

5. Pragma Love: This is the enduring love, based on commitment, patience, and compromise. It's the love that sustains a marriage through challenges.

The Role of Faith

Christian marriage is not just about love between two individuals but also a shared faith. When couples are united in their faith, it strengthens the bond between them. This shared faith becomes the glue that holds the marriage together through life's storms.

Love as a Daily Practice

Love is not a one-time declaration but a daily practice. Christian marriages are built through the small acts of kindness, forgiveness, and grace extended to one another. This means showing love through:

- Communication: Open, honest, and respectful communication is key.
   - Forgiveness: Understanding that both partners are imperfect and will make mistakes.
   - Servanthood: A willingness to serve and support your spouse selflessly.
   - Prayer: Seeking guidance and strength from God through prayer, both individually and as a couple.

Setting the Example

As Christian couples, your marriage should be an example to others, a living testament to the love and grace of God. When others see your healthy, Christ-centered relationship, it can be an inspiration for them.

Conclusion

In this chapter, we've explored the foundation of love as the cornerstone of a Christian marriage. We've seen that Christian love is a complex and multifaceted concept, encompassing selflessness, friendship, passion, and commitment. Faith plays a vital role in maintaining this love, and it's something that you and your spouse will grow in together. As you continue your journey through this book, remember that love is not just a sentiment; it's a daily practice that can transform your home into a place of happiness, peace, and love, reflecting the love of Christ for His Church.

# 2

# The Power of Communication

I ntroduction

Welcome to Chapter 2 of "Healthy Hearts, Happy Homes: A Christian Marriage Handbook." In this chapter, we will delve into the vital aspect of communication within a Christian marriage. Effective communication is the cornerstone of understanding, resolving conflicts, and deepening the bond between spouses.

The Importance of Communication

Effective communication is the lifeblood of a healthy marriage. It allows couples to express their feelings, needs, and desires, while also listening and understanding their spouse's perspective. In a Christian marriage, it's an essential tool for living out the principles of love, empathy, and mutual respect.

Active Listening

One of the key elements of communication is active listening. It involves not just hearing your spouse's words but truly understanding their feelings and point of view. Active listening includes:

- Giving Your Full Attention: Put away distractions and focus on your spouse when they're speaking.

- Empathizing: Try to put yourself in their shoes and understand their emotions.

- Asking Clarifying Questions: If you're not sure, ask for clarification rather than making assumptions.

- Offering Support: Show that you're there to support and help them.

Open and Honest Communication

Honesty is the bedrock of any successful marriage. In a Christian marriage, openness and transparency are particularly important, as truthfulness reflects the love and trust you have for each other. This involves:

- Sharing Your Feelings: Don't keep your emotions bottled up. Share them honestly with your spouse.

- Discussing Concerns: Address issues and concerns promptly, but do so with respect and kindness.

- Avoiding Blame: Instead of blaming, focus on how to work together to find solutions.

- Regular Check-Ins: Periodically set aside time for open conversations about your marriage.

Conflict Resolution

Conflict is a natural part of any relationship, but how it's managed can make or break a marriage. In Christian marriages, conflict resolution should reflect the principles of love, forgiveness, and understanding. Some strategies include:

- Prayer: Seek God's guidance in resolving conflicts and finding solutions.

- Empathy: Try to see the issue from your spouse's perspective.

- Forgiveness: Practice forgiveness as Christ forgave you.

- Seeking Mediation: If necessary, involve a trusted pastor or counselor.

Non-Verbal Communication

Communication isn't just about words. Non-verbal cues, such as body language, tone of voice, and gestures, play a significant role in conveying emotions and intentions. Be mindful of the non-verbal messages you're sending and be attuned to your spouse's non-verbal cues.

Communication Exercises

To improve your communication skills, consider engaging in exercises like active listening practice, journaling, or attending marriage seminars. These activities can help you both grow in your ability to communicate effectively.

Conclusion

Effective communication is the cornerstone of a healthy Christian marriage. It allows you to navigate challenges, express love, and grow together in faith. In this chapter, we've explored the importance of active listening, open and honest communication, conflict resolution, and the role of non-verbal cues in strengthening your connection. Remember that as you communicate, you're not only building a healthier relationship but also reflecting the love and grace of Christ in your marriage.

# 3

# Building Trust and Transparency

I ntroduction

In "Healthy Hearts, Happy Homes: A Christian Marriage Handbook," we recognize the importance of trust and transparency as the pillars of a strong Christian marriage. In this chapter, we'll explore how to cultivate trust and foster transparency in your relationship, creating a secure and loving environment for both spouses.

The Significance of Trust

Trust is the cornerstone of every healthy marriage, and it is built on a foundation of love, commitment, and faith. In a Christian marriage, trust is not only about having faith in your spouse but also in God's plan for your union.

Transparency as a Path to Trust

Transparency is closely linked to trust. It involves open and honest communication about your thoughts, feelings, and actions. Transparency not only reinforces trust but also helps to align your lives and values more closely.

Building Trust and Transparency

1. Honesty and Integrity: Be truthful and maintain your integrity. In every interaction, demonstrate your commitment to a marriage founded on Christian principles.

2. Accountability: Accept responsibility for your actions. In a Christian marriage, accountability is not a burden but an opportunity for growth and grace.

3. Forgiveness: Learn to forgive and seek forgiveness. God's forgiveness is the ultimate example of grace, and it should be mirrored in your marriage.

4. Boundaries: Establish healthy boundaries within your relationship. These boundaries should reflect your values and protect your marriage.

5. Shared Values and Goals: Ensure that your values and long-term goals align. This shared vision can serve as a compass guiding your actions and decisions.

6. Prayer: Seek God's guidance through prayer. Praying together as a couple can help you deepen your trust and strengthen your connection.

Overcoming Challenges

Trust can be tested by life's challenges, such as financial difficulties, health issues, or external pressures. In these moments, it's crucial to rely on your faith and the trust you've built in your spouse. Praying together and seeking support from your Christian community can help you weather these storms together.

Transparency and Intimacy

Transparency is a key component of marital intimacy. By opening up to your spouse about your deepest thoughts, fears, and desires, you foster a level of intimacy that goes beyond the physical. Your spiritual and emotional intimacy can become a powerful force in your Christian marriage.

Building Trust in God

In a Christian marriage, trust extends beyond your spouse to trust in God's plan for your life together. Trust that, even in challenging times, God is present and guiding your path.

Conclusion

In this chapter, we've explored the importance of trust and transparency in building a strong Christian marriage. Trust is not just about having faith in your spouse but also in God's divine plan. Transparency involves open and honest communication and helps align your lives and values. By fostering trust and transparency in your marriage, you're creating a strong foundation that reflects the love, grace, and faith central to Christian relationships. Remember that your trust in God and in each other is the bridge that leads to the healthy, happy home you're striving to build.

# 4

# Nurturing Spiritual Connection

I ntroduction

In "Healthy Hearts, Happy Homes: A Christian Marriage Handbook," we believe that a strong spiritual connection is a vital element of a thriving Christian marriage. This chapter explores the significance of nurturing your spiritual bond and how it can enrich your relationship.

The Role of Spirituality in Marriage

In a Christian marriage, spirituality is the backbone that supports your love, trust, and communication. It's the shared foundation upon which your relationship is built, and it can deepen your connection in profound ways.

Praying Together

Prayer is a powerful way to nurture your spiritual connection. When you and your spouse pray together, you invite God into your marriage, seeking His guidance, wisdom, and blessings. This practice helps you:

- Share Your Hearts: Through prayer, you can openly express your hopes, fears, and dreams to each other and to God.

- Seek Guidance: Prayer can be a source of guidance, helping you make decisions in alignment with your faith.

- Cultivate Gratitude: Thanking God for each other and your blessings can foster appreciation and love in your marriage.

- Find Peace: In times of conflict or stress, prayer can provide a sense of peace and comfort.

Studying Scripture Together

Exploring the Bible as a couple can deepen your spiritual connection. Choose passages or topics that resonate with both of you and reflect on how they apply to your marriage. This shared study can help you:

- Grow in Faith: Understanding and applying Scripture can deepen your faith and commitment to a Christian marriage.

- Unify Your Values: Studying the Bible together helps ensure that your values and beliefs are in sync.

- Find Guidance: Scripture can provide guidance on a wide range of marital issues, from communication to forgiveness.

- Build a Strong Foundation: The wisdom found in the Bible can become the foundation upon which you build your marriage.

Attending Church Together

Regular attendance at your local church is a way to connect with your

Christian community and deepen your faith. Attending church services together can:

- Strengthen Community: By participating in church activities and groups, you create a network of like-minded individuals who can support your marriage.

- Receive Spiritual Teaching: Church services provide an opportunity to receive spiritual guidance and insight.

- Foster Unity: Sharing the experience of worship and fellowship can create a sense of unity in your relationship.

Retreats and Workshops

Consider participating in Christian marriage retreats or workshops. These events provide a dedicated space for you to focus on your spiritual bond, learn new skills, and strengthen your marriage.

Daily Spiritual Practices

Incorporate daily spiritual practices into your routine. These may include individual devotions, grace before meals, or bedtime prayers with your spouse.

Conclusion

Nurturing your spiritual connection is a fundamental aspect of a Christian marriage. By praying together, studying Scripture, attending church, and participating in spiritual activities, you are not only deepening your faith but also strengthening your bond as a couple. Remember, it's the spiritual connection that will sustain your marriage through every season, as it's grounded in the enduring love and wisdom of God. Your shared faith is the foundation for a healthy, happy home built on Christian principles.

# 5

# The Dance of Compromise and Forgiveness

Introduction

In "Healthy Hearts, Happy Homes: A Christian Marriage Handbook," we recognize that compromise and forgiveness are essential elements of a thriving Christian marriage. This chapter explores how to navigate the delicate dance of compromise and forgiveness, fostering a harmonious and loving relationship.

The Importance of Compromise

Compromise is not a sign of weakness but a testament to the strength of your love and the foundation of your Christian marriage. It's a willingness to put the needs and desires of your spouse on par with your own, seeking harmony and balance in your relationship.

Balancing Individual Needs

In a Christian marriage, it's essential to balance individual needs and desires with those of the partnership. This requires open communication and a heart willing to listen and adjust.

The Role of Forgiveness

Forgiveness is a divine act of love and grace that mirrors God's forgiveness of His children. In a Christian marriage, forgiveness allows you to move past mistakes, offering a chance for renewal and reconciliation.

Practical Steps in Compromise and Forgiveness

1. Open and Respectful Dialogue: Engage in honest, respectful conversations to understand each other's viewpoints and negotiate compromises.

2. Prioritize: Distinguish between wants and needs, prioritizing what truly matters in the grand scheme of your marriage.

3. Meet in the Middle: Compromise often involves meeting in the middle, finding a solution that satisfies both partners.

4. Forgiveness Rituals: Develop rituals or practices that signify forgiveness and renewal. For instance, you might say a prayer together or engage in a meaningful gesture.

5. Letting Go of Resentment: Forgiveness involves letting go of resentment and the desire for revenge.

6. Seeking Counseling: In situations where compromise and forgiveness are challenging, consider seeking the guidance of a Christian counselor or pastor.

The Healing Power of Forgiveness

Forgiveness is a powerful healer in a Christian marriage. It can mend broken trust, soothe emotional wounds, and enable a fresh start. The act of forgiveness is closely tied to your faith in Christ's redemptive power and His teachings on love and mercy.

Grace and Growth

In a Christian marriage, understanding the concept of grace is essential. Grace is the undeserved love and favor that God extends to us, and it should be mirrored in your marriage. It allows room for growth and transformation, fostering a loving environment where both spouses can evolve and improve.

The Journey of Compromise and Forgiveness

Remember that the dance of compromise and forgiveness is an ongoing journey. It's about continuous learning, understanding, and demonstrating Christ-like love. Through this journey, your marriage can become a beautiful testimony to the grace, love, and forgiveness found in your faith.

Conclusion

Compromise and forgiveness are the threads that weave together the fabric of a harmonious Christian marriage. By embracing the spirit of compromise, you can find solutions that honor both partners' needs and desires. Forgiveness allows your relationship to heal, grow, and thrive. In both, you're living out the principles of love, grace, and humility that Christ exemplified in His teachings. These acts of compromise and forgiveness create a home where healthy hearts and happy homes flourish.

# 6

# Cherishing Intimacy and Romance

Introduction

In "Healthy Hearts, Happy Homes: A Christian Marriage Handbook," we understand that maintaining intimacy and romance is crucial for a strong and enduring Christian marriage. This chapter delves into the importance of nurturing these aspects of your relationship and provides guidance on keeping the spark alive.

The Role of Intimacy

Intimacy goes beyond the physical aspect of a relationship. It encompasses emotional connection, trust, and spiritual closeness. In a Christian marriage, cultivating intimacy strengthens your bond and deepens your love.

The Importance of Romance

Romance is the art of keeping the flame of love burning bright. It's the conscious effort to show your affection and appreciation for your spouse. In a Christian marriage, romance is a beautiful way to mirror God's love for His children.

Nurturing Intimacy

1. Open Communication: Share your thoughts, feelings, and desires with your spouse. Create an atmosphere where you can be completely open and vulnerable.

2. Quality Time: Make time for each other regularly. Schedule dates, even in the midst of a busy life, to ensure that you're nurturing your connection.

3. Shared Devotions: Reading the Bible and praying together not only deepens your faith but also strengthens your spiritual connection.

4. Acts of Service: Show love through actions that express thoughtfulness and care, such as making breakfast in bed, preparing a surprise dinner, or handling chores for your spouse.

5. Physical Affection: Physical touch is essential for intimacy. Hold hands, hug, and share moments of physical closeness.

Cultivating Romance

1. Love Letters: Write heartfelt letters to your spouse, expressing your love, appreciation, and affection.

2. Surprises: Plan surprises to keep the romance alive. This might include unexpected gifts, love notes, or special date nights.

3. Date Nights: Continue to date your spouse, even after years of marriage. Dedicate time to spend quality moments together.

4. Expressing Affection: Verbalize your love and appreciation. Express

compliments and words of affection regularly.

5. Spontaneity: Embrace spontaneous acts of love and romance to keep the relationship fresh and exciting.

Overcoming Challenges

Intimacy and romance may face challenges in a Christian marriage, such as stress, work, or raising children. Overcoming these obstacles requires prioritizing your relationship, being creative, and communicating openly.

The Sanctity of Marriage

Your Christian marriage is a sacred covenant. Cherishing intimacy and romance not only strengthens your relationship but also reflects the sanctity of marriage in the eyes of God.

Conclusion

Nurturing intimacy and keeping the flame of romance alive is a continuous journey in a Christian marriage. It's about maintaining the love, affection, and connection that initially brought you together. By investing in these aspects of your relationship, you're honoring your covenant with God and creating a healthy, happy home filled with love and joy. Intimacy and romance are the threads that make your love story beautifully unique.

# 7

# Embracing Challenges and Growing Together

Introduction

In "Healthy Hearts, Happy Homes: A Christian Marriage Handbook," we understand that life's challenges are inevitable. In this chapter, we will explore the importance of embracing these challenges and using them as opportunities for growth in your Christian marriage.

The Inevitability of Challenges

Life is a journey filled with ups and downs, and no marriage is exempt from challenges. However, in a Christian marriage, these challenges can serve as opportunities for you and your spouse to draw closer to each other and to God.

The Role of Faith

In times of adversity, your faith plays a crucial role in sustaining your marriage.

It's during these moments that your trust in God and your shared spiritual connection can provide strength and resilience.

Approaching Challenges Together

Facing challenges together is a testament to the unity of your marriage. Instead of viewing obstacles as something that drives you apart, look at them as opportunities to deepen your bond. Some strategies include:

- Open Communication: Share your feelings and concerns with your spouse. Discuss the challenges openly and honestly.

- Prayer: Seek guidance and strength through prayer, both individually and as a couple.

- Seeking Support: Don't hesitate to reach out to your Christian community, a pastor, or a counselor for support and guidance.

- Forgiveness: Remember the importance of forgiveness, as it's often necessary during challenging times.

- Adapting and Learning: Use challenges as opportunities for personal growth and growth as a couple.

Specific Challenges

1. Financial Challenges: Money can be a source of stress in a marriage. Work together on a budget, set financial goals, and communicate openly about financial matters.

2. Parenting Challenges: Raising children can be both rewarding and challenging. Make sure you are on the same page when it comes to parenting values and approaches.

3. Health Challenges: Illness or health issues can be emotionally and physically taxing. Support each other with love, care, and empathy.

4. Work-Life Balance: Finding a healthy balance between work and personal life is essential. Ensure that you allocate quality time to your marriage.

The Role of Resilience

Resilience is the ability to bounce back from adversity. In a Christian marriage, it's the determination to persevere through the trials, knowing that God is with you every step of the way.

Growth Through Challenges

Challenges can be a catalyst for personal and marital growth. As you navigate these difficulties together, you become a stronger, wiser, and more compassionate couple.

Celebrating Victories

Don't forget to celebrate your victories together. These moments of triumph, both small and large, are reminders of your strength and resilience in Christ.

Conclusion

Embracing challenges and growing together is an integral part of a Christian marriage. Challenges are opportunities for you to lean on your faith, trust in God's plan, and draw closer to your spouse. By facing adversity with resilience, open communication, and a shared sense of purpose, you can navigate life's trials and emerge from them even stronger. In the end, it's these shared experiences that help build a healthy, happy home filled with love and the grace of God.

# 8

# Cultivating a Legacy of Love

I ntroduction

In "Healthy Hearts, Happy Homes: A Christian Marriage Handbook," we understand that a strong Christian marriage is not only about the present but also about leaving a legacy of love for generations to come. In this chapter, we explore how you can cultivate a lasting and meaningful legacy that reflects the values of your faith.

The Power of Legacy

A legacy is the enduring impact you leave behind, and in a Christian marriage, it's a testament to the love, faith, and commitment that have been the foundation of your relationship.

The Role of Love and Faith

Love and faith are the pillars of your legacy. The love you've shared and the faith that has sustained your marriage can serve as a beacon of inspiration for your family and community.

Passing on Values

Your legacy involves passing on not only material possessions but also the values, beliefs, and principles that have defined your marriage. Some key aspects include:

- Christian Faith: Instilling a strong faith in God and the teachings of Jesus Christ.

- Love and Forgiveness: Encouraging love, forgiveness, and grace as central tenets of family life.

- Service and Compassion: Teaching the importance of serving others and showing compassion to those in need.

- Open Communication: Demonstrating the value of open and honest communication within a family.

Modeling a Healthy Marriage

Your marriage serves as a model for your children and others in your community. As you navigate the challenges and joys of your relationship, you set an example of how to build and maintain a strong, loving Christian marriage.

Legacy-Building Practices

1. Family Devotions: Incorporate regular family devotions into your routine, reading the Bible and praying together.

2. Sharing Family Stories: Share stories about your journey as a couple, including both your challenges and triumphs.

3. Service Projects: Engage in community service projects as a family to demonstrate the importance of giving back.

4. Quality Time: Dedicate quality time to your children, engaging in meaningful conversations and creating lasting memories.

5. Parenting with Love and Grace: Model a loving, grace-filled approach to parenting, emphasizing understanding and forgiveness.

Passing on Traditions

Cultivate family traditions that reflect your Christian values. These traditions can become the threads that tie your family together across generations.

Teaching the Next Generation

Through your words and actions, you can teach your children and grandchildren the importance of love, faith, and commitment in a Christian marriage. Be intentional about passing on these values.

Conclusion

Cultivating a legacy of love is a profound and fulfilling part of a Christian marriage. Your legacy is a testament to the enduring power of love, faith, and commitment in your relationship. As you pass on your values, model a healthy marriage, and teach the next generation, you're leaving a lasting impact on your family and community. Your legacy will be a source of inspiration, guidance, and love for generations to come, reflecting the grace and blessings of God in your marriage.

# 9

# Sustaining Love Through the Seasons of Life

I ntroduction

In "Healthy Hearts, Happy Homes: A Christian Marriage Handbook," we understand that love is not static, but rather it evolves and deepens as you journey through life. This chapter explores how to sustain love in your Christian marriage through all the seasons of life, adapting and growing together.

The Ever-Changing Seasons of Life

Life is a series of seasons, each with its unique challenges and blessings. These seasons may include the early years of marriage, the arrival of children, career changes, and retirement, among others. In a Christian marriage, it's important to navigate these seasons with love, faith, and unity.

A Foundation of Love

The foundation of your marriage, built on love, trust, and faith, is what will sustain you through the changing seasons. The love you share should be a constant, regardless of external circumstances.

Flexibility and Adaptation

Adapting to different seasons requires flexibility. As a couple, you must be willing to adjust, compromise, and grow together, all while maintaining the core values of your Christian faith.

Embracing New Beginnings

1. The Early Years of Marriage: In this season, focus on building a strong foundation. Invest time in getting to know each other, communicating openly, and nurturing your love.

2. Parenthood: Welcoming children into your lives is a time of joy and adjustment. Be a team in parenting, prioritize your marriage, and maintain open communication.

3. Empty Nesting: As your children grow and leave the home, it's an opportunity to rediscover each other and rekindle your romance.

4. Career Changes: Career shifts can be both exciting and challenging. Support each other's ambitions, while still nurturing your marriage.

5. Retirement: In this season, you have more time for each other. Explore new interests and activities together, deepening your connection.

Resilience Through Challenges

Life's seasons may also include trials and difficulties, such as health issues or financial struggles. Approach these challenges as opportunities to lean on your faith and to grow closer to each other.

Sustaining Love and Faith

Your Christian faith is a constant anchor through life's ever-changing seasons. It's important to maintain your relationship with God and to turn to Him for guidance and support.

The Beauty of a Lifelong Journey

A Christian marriage is a lifelong journey filled with love, grace, and faith. It's a testament to God's enduring love, and as you move through the seasons of life, your marriage can become a shining example of the beauty of love that grows and deepens with each passing year.

Conclusion

Sustaining love through the seasons of life is an integral part of a Christian marriage. By embracing change with love, faith, and unity, you're ensuring that your relationship remains strong and enduring. Through every season, you're not only enriching your marriage but also exemplifying the enduring love and grace of God in your lives. Remember that your love story is a testament to the beauty of a Christian marriage that thrives in all seasons.

# 10

# Celebrating Milestones and Renewing Vows

I ntroduction

In "Healthy Hearts, Happy Homes: A Christian Marriage Handbook," we understand the significance of celebrating milestones in your marriage journey. This chapter explores the importance of acknowledging your achievements, cherishing your love, and renewing your vows to strengthen your Christian marriage.

The Significance of Milestones

Milestones are moments of reflection and celebration in your marriage. They offer you an opportunity to look back on your journey, appreciate how far you've come, and set intentions for the future.

The Power of Celebration

Celebrating milestones is a chance to honor your love, perseverance, and the grace of God that has been with you throughout your marriage. It's a joyful recognition of your journey together.

Acknowledging Achievements

Each milestone in your marriage, whether it's your first year together, a significant anniversary, or overcoming a challenging time, is an achievement. Acknowledging these accomplishments is a way of valuing your partnership.

Renewing Vows

Renewing your vows is a powerful way to reaffirm your love, faith, and commitment to each other. It's an opportunity to revisit the promises you made on your wedding day and to make new promises that reflect your growth as a couple.

Celebratory Practices

1. Anniversaries: Celebrate your wedding anniversary as a time to reflect on the past year and set intentions for the future. Consider planning a special date or getaway.

2. Renewal of Vows: Hold a ceremony to renew your vows, either privately or with friends and family. It's an opportunity to express your love and commitment.

3. Reflective Rituals: Create personal rituals that help you reflect on your marriage journey, such as reading your original wedding vows together or revisiting letters you've written to each other.

4. Legacy Building: Continue the legacy-building practices you've established, passing on your values and traditions to the next generation.

## The Power of Gratitude

Practicing gratitude for your partner and your marriage is an essential part of celebrating milestones. Expressing thankfulness for the love and support you've received strengthens your bond and appreciation for each other.

## Setting New Intentions

With each milestone, set new intentions for your marriage. Consider what you want to achieve in the coming year or in the next phase of your journey. These intentions can be spiritual, personal, or relationship-focused.

## The Role of Your Christian Faith

In your Christian marriage, your faith remains a guiding force in the celebration of milestones and renewal of vows. It's a constant source of love, grace, and inspiration for the future.

## Conclusion

Celebrating milestones and renewing vows is an essential practice in a Christian marriage. It's a time to cherish your love, acknowledge your achievements, and set intentions for the future. By embracing these practices, you're not only celebrating your journey but also reaffirming your commitment to a life filled with love and faith. Your Christian marriage is a testament to the enduring power of God's grace, and each milestone is a reminder of the blessings and joy that love and faith bring to your home.

# 11

# Strengthening Your Marriage Through Prayer

Introduction

In "Healthy Hearts, Happy Homes: A Christian Marriage Handbook," we understand that prayer is a powerful tool to strengthen and sustain a Christian marriage. This chapter explores the significance of prayer in your relationship and provides guidance on incorporating prayer into your daily lives.

The Power of Prayer

Prayer is a direct line of communication with God. In a Christian marriage, it can serve as a spiritual anchor, fostering unity, love, and trust between spouses.

The Role of Prayer in Marriage

Prayer plays several vital roles in your marriage:

- Connection: It connects you and your spouse to God, strengthening your shared faith.

- Communication: It encourages open and honest communication with each other and with God.

- Guidance: It seeks God's guidance and wisdom for your relationship.

- Gratitude: It fosters an attitude of thankfulness for each other and your blessings.

Praying Together

Praying together as a couple is a powerful practice that deepens your spiritual connection. Some ways to incorporate prayer into your marriage include:

- Morning Prayer: Begin your day with a simple prayer of gratitude and for God's guidance throughout the day.

- Mealtime Prayer: Say grace before meals, thanking God for the provision and sharing a moment of reflection.

- Bedtime Prayer: Conclude your day with a prayer, reflecting on your blessings and challenges.

- Weekly or Monthly Devotions: Dedicate time for more extended devotions as a couple, reading the Bible and praying together.

Individual Prayer

In addition to praying together, it's essential for each spouse to have their individual prayer life. This personal connection with God allows you to bring your individual needs, concerns, and thanksgiving to Him.

The Prayer of Intercession

Intercessory prayer is when you pray for your spouse, seeking God's blessings, guidance, and protection on their behalf. This practice reflects your love and care for each other.

Prayer for Your Marriage

Specifically praying for your marriage is a way to invite God's grace into your relationship. Seek guidance on how to love, support, and nurture your marriage. This practice can help you overcome challenges and deepen your connection.

Prayer for Your Family

Include your family in your prayers. Praying for your children and their well-being, your extended family, and your Christian community reflects the importance of faith and community in your marriage.

Praying Through Challenges

When faced with difficulties, turn to prayer as a source of strength and guidance. Praying together during challenging times can help you overcome obstacles and grow closer in faith.

Conclusion

Incorporating prayer into your marriage is a powerful way to strengthen your connection, deepen your faith, and invite God's presence into your relationship. Prayer is a practice that reflects the core principles of love, faith, and trust in a Christian marriage. By making prayer a central part of your lives, you're nurturing a healthy, happy home founded on the grace and blessings of God. Your prayers are a testimony to the enduring power of love and faith in your marriage.

# 12

# Building a Supportive Community

I ntroduction

In "Healthy Hearts, Happy Homes: A Christian Marriage Handbook," we understand that a strong support system is essential for a thriving Christian marriage. This chapter explores the significance of building a supportive community and provides guidance on how to nurture these relationships.

The Importance of Community

In a Christian marriage, a supportive community offers strength, guidance, and love. This community can include family, friends, fellow church members, and others who share your faith.

Building Supportive Relationships

1. Family: Engage with both your immediate and extended family as they play a crucial role in providing support and a sense of belonging.

2. Church Community: Active participation in your church community fosters connections with like-minded individuals who can offer guidance and encouragement.

3. Friendships: Cherish your friendships, especially those with couples who share your values and can relate to the joys and challenges of marriage.

4. Mentorship: Seek guidance and mentorship from older, wiser couples who can offer insights and support in your marital journey.

5. Support Groups: Consider joining support groups specifically designed for married couples, where you can share experiences and learn from others.

Nurturing Your Relationships

Building supportive relationships requires effort and intention. Some strategies include:

- Open Communication: Be open and honest in your interactions, sharing your thoughts and concerns.

- Quality Time: Spend quality time with friends and family, deepening your connections.

- Acts of Service: Show love and care by offering help and support when needed.

- Attending Church Activities: Participate in church events and activities to strengthen your connection with your church community.

Seeking Guidance

In challenging times, it's important to seek guidance and support from your community. Your pastor or a Christian counselor can offer valuable insights and advice.

Boundaries

While building a supportive community is essential, it's equally crucial to establish healthy boundaries. These boundaries protect your marriage and help maintain a balance between your community and your relationship.

Sharing Your Journey

Share your marital journey with your supportive community. Be open about your successes, challenges, and the role your faith plays in your relationship. Your experiences can offer inspiration and guidance to others.

Conclusion

Building a supportive community is an integral part of a Christian marriage. It provides strength, guidance, and love when you need it most. Your community is a reflection of the love and grace of God, and it plays a significant role in nurturing a healthy, happy home. By fostering these relationships, you're building a network of support that can sustain your marriage through every season of life. Remember that your community is a testament to the enduring power of love, faith, and unity in your Christian marriage.

Book Summary: Healthy Hearts, Happy Homes - A Christian Marriage Handbook

"Healthy Hearts, Happy Homes: A Christian Marriage Handbook" is a comprehensive guide to building and sustaining a strong, faith-centered marriage. This book, written with the wisdom of Christian principles, offers invaluable insights and practical advice for couples at all stages of their marital journey.

The book is divided into twelve chapters, each addressing a crucial aspect of a Christian marriage, and is centered on the core principles of love, faith, and unity. Here's an overview of the book's key themes:

1.   Chapter 1: Foundations of Love and Faith: The book begins by emphasizing the significance of love and faith as the bedrock of a Christian marriage. It discusses the importance of aligning your values and faith to establish a firm foundation.

2. Chapter 2: Effective Communication: Effective communication is the cornerstone of a successful marriage. This chapter explores techniques for open, honest, and compassionate communication.

3. Chapter 3: Trust and Forgiveness: Trust and forgiveness are explored as essential elements for a thriving marriage. The chapter delves into how trust is built and how forgiveness can heal and strengthen a relationship.

4. Chapter 4: Nurturing Spiritual Connection: A strong spiritual connection is vital in a Christian marriage. This section discusses the significance of praying together, studying Scripture, and attending church to deepen this bond.

5. Chapter 5: The Dance of Compromise and Forgiveness: Compromise and forgiveness are essential for a harmonious marriage. This chapter offers practical steps to navigate these crucial aspects of a Christian relationship.

6. Chapter 6: Cherishing Intimacy and Romance: Intimacy and romance are explored as ways to keep the spark alive in a Christian marriage. The chapter provides suggestions for nurturing emotional and physical closeness.

7.  Chapter 7: Embracing Challenges and Growing Together: The book

acknowledges that challenges are inevitable and should be embraced as opportunities for growth, with resilience and faith as the guiding principles.

8. Chapter 8: Cultivating a Legacy of Love: This chapter discusses the significance of leaving a lasting legacy of love, faith, and values for future generations, focusing on the role of family traditions and values.

9. Chapter 9: Sustaining Love Through the Seasons of Life: The book highlights the importance of adapting and growing together through various seasons of life, including the early years of marriage, parenthood, and retirement.

10. Chapter 10: Celebrating Milestones and Renewing Vows: The value of celebrating achievements and renewing vows is explored as a way to honor the journey and reaffirm love and commitment.

11. Chapter 11: Strengthening Your Marriage Through Prayer: Prayer is presented as a powerful tool for deepening the spiritual connection in a Christian marriage. The chapter offers insights into incorporating prayer into daily life and relationship.

12. Chapter 12: Building a Supportive Community: The book concludes by emphasizing the importance of a strong support system, including family, friends, and church community. It provides guidance on building and nurturing these vital relationships.

"Healthy Hearts, Happy Homes" is a guide for Christian couples seeking to cultivate a lasting, faith-based marriage. It underscores the enduring power of love, faith, and unity and offers practical strategies for building a relationship rooted in Christian principles. This handbook serves as a valuable resource for couples to create and maintain a healthy, happy home centered around their shared Christian faith.

www.ingramcontent.com/pod-product-compliance
Lightning Source LLC
Chambersburg PA
CBHW051053060526
44539CB00047B/1625